QUIET PLEASE

By Richard Flint

$\mathcal{P}$
$\mathcal{L}$
$\mathcal{P}$

Pendelton Lane Publishing
West Palm Beach, Florida

To Karen
  Whose purpose in my life
  is now something I understand

Quiet please
   I'm tired of listening

Quiet please
   I'm tired of people

Quiet please
   I'm tired of interruptions

Quiet please
   I need some silence
       Some moments that are unstructured

Some time when I don't have to think,
              to respond,
              to be a part of anything

Time when I can drift,
                can relax
            can goof-off
         without feeling
                or being made
         to feel guilty

Quiet please
        this life is in need of repair
    Repair that cannot be done by
                another person
    Repair that can only be handled
                alone—
                        by me

Quiet please
    Life undergoing maintenance.

Do you know what
   I miss most in our relationship

The quiet times
   we used to have

Remember when we would sit for hours
   and just talk
               many times not about
                   anything in particular
we would just visit
               Remember how much we
               learned about each other
we always had time to talk
                   Now,
               we don't take the time

I know we're busy
   I know we're tired
         but oh,
how I long for the times
         when we just chatted

Remember how we would go for walks
or just sit out under the stars
how we would hold hands
and enjoy our own
definitions to romance
Now
it's rare if we touch
we have no time to walk
to watch the stars
to hold each other

Maybe
just maybe
I'm a silly romantic
but romance is so important to me
to me it
defines touch
defines closeness
defines love

Honey,
what has happened to us
we've said we would not
become like other couples
but look at us
we're not different
we've become boring like the others

Let's recapture what we had
I know you can't go back
but

    we can review
      re-define
  re-direct our energies
    our priorities

Let's not lose
    the joy of us.

I often find myself
    wondering about death
I wonder
    what is it
        is that all there is to a life
We are born
        for what
                to die
What do we leave behind
        besides a plot of earth
            where they place our remains

I don't want to simply
    be a mound of earth
I want to be more
    I want to live on
        after this body is gone
I want to live on
    in the minds of people
I want to live on
    in the lives of people

I want my thoughts
    to be lasting reflections
I want my words
    to be continual strength

I want my understandings
to offer direction
I don't want a grave
to be the end
maybe a pause
but not a period for
the meaning of my life
I want to be tomorrow
even if *I* am not today.

May I never forget
that tears
are God's way of making sure
that our lives
don't flood.

Hey —
     where am I
          I don't recognize this place
     who am I,
          I'm not sure anymore
     how did I get here,
          I can't remember
     when did I arrive,
          why am I here

Oh please
     somebody help me
I'm trapped on this merry-go-round
     and,
               it won't slow down
                    oh no —
                    it's spinning faster now

Hey you
          I know you
               will you help me
No
     please don't leave
               come back
                    please come back
          where did he go
     why did he run away

Somebody
   please help me
  I'm getting dizzy
    from this merry-go-round

I know there has got to be
    a switch
   that controls this
but
  why can't I see it
   why is it not there
  why can't I turn
      it off

Hey you —
  please help me
     why are you laughing
  this is not funny
   this frightens me

No —
  don't leave
   please come back
  Help me —
   I can't take much more

Why is it
    when you need help the most
                            that
        you can't find it

Why is it
    that when the real moments
                    of struggle
        are upon you
You've got to face them alone

You know —
    maybe
        just maybe
    I'm too dependent on others

Maybe
    Just maybe
        rather than calling for help
            I should
                search for the solution

Maybe
just maybe
I can do it
myself
and
in doing it myself
I will learn
that the switches of life
are inside
not hidden
on the wall.

Let me tell you something
     you'll never hurt me again
I can't believe I let you treat me that way
     I can't believe
          I let you abuse me

You have pushed
               my tolerance
                    my patience
                         my understanding
                              my love
          to the breaking point

I've tried to be patient
               and understanding
     because I do care
               and
               I didn't want to hurt you
but enough
     is enough
you haven't cared who you hurt
     you think only of yourself
you've felt you could do anything you've wanted
          and
               I'd be there waiting

Well my friend —
   it's time you learned the real facts of life
   I'm not your doormat

I'm not your possession
         I'm not your punching bag

I'm me
   and
         I've had enough of you

From now on —
   I'll make the rules

From now on —
   you don't matter

From now on —
   I'll think of me first

Rule #1
   Goodbye
      and
         don't come begging

You've had every chance in the book
　　and
　　　　you've abused them all
　　　　　now —
　　　　　　　there are no more chances

Hey —
　　how does it feel
　　　　For me
　　　　　it's great

No longer am I your puppet
　　that jumps when you
　　　　pull the string

No longer am I your possession
　　for you to use and abuse
　　　　whenever you want

No longer am I your cleaning person
　　who works without pay or thanks

Guess who I am
　　I'm me
　　　and
　　　　it feels
　　　　　　　GREAT!

Hey —
　　I'm
　　　　sorry

I

　　screamed
　　　　at
　　　　　　you
　　　　　　　　because
　　I
　　wasn't
　　　　mature
　　　　　　enough
　　　　　　　to
　　　　　　　　scream
　　　　　　　　　at
　　　　　　　　　　myself

I'm sorry.

Sometimes you really leave me
                      feeling lost
You say things
              and
                    I have no idea where
          you get them

Sometimes your thoughts,
                  your words
        eat at my patience
              I try so hard to listen
                  with objectivity
          to what you say
                      but
when you speak out of the pain
            that others have created
                I have not
                    am not
          a part of that experience
yet —
          you dump it on me

Why —
        why do you do that
                when I am the one person
who works to let you be you
        the one person
                who accepts the real you
        the one person
                who sets you free

Stop a moment
        look at what you're doing

Stop a moment
        look at who you're doing it to

Stop a moment
        why are you doing it to me

Don't you see what you're doing
        can't you see —
                you're pushing me away
                Don't you care

Stop a moment
        Pay attention to what you're doing.

Guess what
    I'm nervous about seeing you

Even after the numbers of times
        we have been together
            I still get those
        little butterflies inside

I feel like a little child
    waiting
        anticipating
            eager for
        the expected surprise
                It's such a
        neat feeling

I want to laugh
        and cry
    at the same time

I think if I ever lose
    this nervousness
        I will worry about us

It helps me understand
    how much you mean to my life
        how much I am in love with you

19

Wow —
   I'm nervous

            I'm glad.

I needed you last night
                        and
            you were nowhere around

*F*or the first time
            in a long time

I was not only lonely for you
            but
                        I was alone for you

*Y*es —
            I've missed you before
                        but

                                    never —
            never, like last night

*B*efore I knew it
            I was scared
        I had never felt
                    that alone before
            it was a void
                        that only you
            could fill

Before I could stop it
                I was crying
                        not tears
        but,
                emotions

Emotions that were confusing

I was crying
                because I missed you

You were nowhere
                to touch
                        to hear

I was crying
                because I felt alone

Before I've been able to
                touch you mentally
        but —
                this time my mind lost you
                        and
                                I panicked

I was crying
    because *I* wanted you
I realized again
    how much *I* love you
How much you
    are a part of my life
How much you
    mean to my life

Last night I needed you
    and
    you were nowhere
    to be found.

Would you tell me that
you miss me

I need to hear those words
right now

I feel alone
and feel no one really cares
about me

Sometimes we just need to feel
that someone misses us
that someone cares

Would you tell me that
you love me

I really need to hear those words
right now

You see —
I don't feel very loveable
right now

I feel a void inside
as if I am totally alone
as if I am the only one here

I need to know I'm not alone
    I need to know someone cares
        someone loves me

Would you tell me that
        I'm special

I really need to hear those words
              Right now

I don't feel special
    I feel less than valuable
      I feel like a speck
        in a world of dots

I need to know I am not
        a nothing
    I need to hear
        I'm special

Does all this sound strange
    I'm just confused right now

I'm not sure about
      a lot of things
        I need you
      to touch my life

You are my calm wind
   When I feel like a rushing storm

You are my compass
   in the midst of my jungle

You are my blanket of warmth
   in the midst of my moments of coldness

You are the only voice I want to hear
   when the whole world is screaming

You are my adventure
   in the midst of sameness

You are my definition
      of meaningfulness.

I have a question for you
    Why did we fight last night
        What happened

The evening was going so great
    We went shopping
        We had supper
            We walked
                We talked
                We held each other
            We kissed
        We wanted each other

Then things changed
    Why?
        What happened

How could such a great beginning
    have such a meaningless ending

How could we let it happen
    an innocent word
        spoken in jest

A reaction
        and then —
    an evening that had been created
            destroyed

Hey —
　let's not let that
　　happen again

Those evenings are too special
　to allow them to be
　　　　　taken away

Say —
　can we learn from last night
　　　　　and
　　try again tonight.

I know you're not
    going to like this
                but,
        I've got to say it

I'm not Tom
    I don't look like him
        I don't sound like him
            I don't treat you like he did

I'm not Tom
        and
    I don't appreciate
            being compared to him

I know
    I understand
        he was a part of your life

The two of you grew-up together
    you shared two children
        I know
            I understand
        those are important events
but, please
    please note the verbs are
                            past tense

When are you going to do
the same with him

Do you understand how difficult it is
to sit and listen to you talk
about Tom

Hey,
what about us

Is the present more important
than the past

If so —
why not treat it so
For if your past
is more important
than your present

What am I doing here

I'm not saying this to hurt you
I'm only trying to help you

Understand what you're doing
to yourself
to us.

I'm trying to be patient
but honey
I'm not Tom
and
I'm tired of living with him

I'm tired
of sharing you with him
I'm not Tom
I'm me.

The
    hardest
        points
           in
              life

are
   not
      giving-up
          but
            turning
              loose.

It is hard to move from this house
    It's part of me

Well
        it's empty now

All the furniture is gone
        Everyone has left
                    Old friend
            please don't hate me

I don't want to leave
                I have no choice

I think I'll sit here for one more moment
            and listen
        I can still hear the sounds
            of this my home

It's hard to leave this place
    It's been my security
            my companion
                my refuge
                    my escape

But —
        I must go now
            I'll continue to cry
                I'll continue to miss this place

Don't worry —
        You'll always be a part of my life

It was hard to move from this place
    It was difficult
        watching them carry things out

I wanted to scream at them
    I wanted to run over
            grab the items
                and place them back
        where they belong

It was hard to move today
    Oh, what memories this place holds
        some that make you smile
            some that make you laugh
                some that make you cry

This house has experienced so much with me
    It knows more of the real me
        than any person

They tell me —
        don't fret
    after all —
        it's only a house

They don't know what this house means to me
    They don't understand that we're friends

They don't care about this house
            the way I do.
        It's hard
            to say good-bye to a friend

Good-bye, old friend
    It's hard to leave this place
                    but
                I must shut the door
        file the memories
        and move forward

For I know
        the next place is waiting

But God —
    is it hard to accept
                turn loose
    and move on.

I sit here tonight
    and watch you sleep

*Y*our body all nestled
    and curled up
        under the sheets

I sit here tonight
        and watch you sleep

and *I* think
    how lucky *I* am
        to have you in my life
    you add so much meaning
        to my directions

I think —
    how beautiful you are
not just outwardly
        but from the inside

*Y*our beauty glows from the inside
    you leave a little of yourself
        in everything you touch
           including me

$\mathcal{I}$ think —
    how much $\mathcal{I}$ am in love with you
      how that has grown
    how special you make me feel
how easy it is to love you

$\mathcal{I}$ sit here tonight
    and watch you sleep
how peaceful you look
      and $\mathcal{I}$ know
    how much peace you have
      brought to my life

$\mathcal{Y}$ou came along
    when $\mathcal{I}$ wasn't looking
and filled a room of my life
    that was vacant
    that needed redecorating
that had been damaged
    by the prior tenant

$\mathcal{Y}$ou came along
    didn't force your way in
    but —
      in your own way
let me discover that
    you were right for that room

I sit here tonight
   and watch you sleep

*K*nowing that I
     am one of the luckiest
   people in the world

*R*est well, my love.

Thanks for reminding me
    that it's okay to still be
           a child

Sometimes I forget that

Sometimes I take life too serious
    I forget to jump in the mud puddles

Sometimes I move at such a fast pace
    I forget to watch the bugs play

Sometimes I get so involved in work
    I forget to visit the playground

Sometimes I'm so busy being an adult
    I forget about being a child

Thanks for reminding me
    that it's okay to be a child

Do you know how long it's been
    since I

        swang on a swing
           played on a slide
    went up and down on a teeter totter
           played hopscotch
           took the time
              to visit the playground

Thanks for reminding me
that it's okay to be a child

Hey —
do me a favor
keep reminding me

Isn't it interesting
how soon we forget.

I love the early morning
                    before the world wakes up

I love the early morning
          before its silence is interrupted
                    with the sounds
of people changing its
                              early morning pace

*I*sn't it interesting
          that the early morning
                    is about the only time you
          can hear the birds sing
          the wind blow
                    the flowers stretch
                         the sun pop up
          to say an energetic
                              Good morning

I love the early morning
                    before the world wakes up
because —
                    it's my time

*T*here are no phones
               to ring in my ears

There are no humans
        to interrupt my thoughts

No unwelcome guests
        who need me

I love the early morning
        before the world wakes up

It's a special time
        of energy
            of thought
                of aloneness

It's a special time
        of growth

For you
    can direct your energy

You can channel your thoughts
    you can be alone
        with just you

I love the early morning
    before the world wakes up.

Why are you here just now
    I know you are a stranger

One I have never met before
            yet —
                I have

You are not her
            but you look just like her
    It's so weird
            For so long she was gone
                she had chosen to leave

Now —
    out of the blue
            she returns

Why I ask
    I was over her

I had filed her in the memories of life
        Then she calls
                Just like nothing had happened

She walks back in
        I tell myself—No
    I won't let her back

Then —
　　　you appear

I don't know you
　　　　　but —
　　　　　　　you make me think of her

Please, go away
　　　Please, let me close my eyes
　　　　　and you disappear

I don't need this now
　　　I don't need the wounds
　　　　　re-opened

I need more time to heal
　　　I need time
　　　　　to forget
　　　　　　to forgive
　　　　　to sort out
　　　to try and understand.

How could you hurt me like that
All I've ever asked,
All I've ever wanted
was to be loved by you

How could you do what
you knew would hurt me

You've said you loved me
and only me
Why then did you
need him

Haven't I been good to you
Haven't I shown you
that I love you
Haven't I worked
to make you happy

I've put every bit of energy I have
into this relationship

I've even sacrificed my
personal dreams for you

For what
For this

Answer me —
        please answer me

What have I done
        to deserve this
Have I hurt you
        Have I been unfaithful to you
        Have I not tried

How could you do what
        you knew would hurt me

You've said
        it was nothing
it was only a weak moment
that
        it's over

Don't you understand
        That's not the point

You did it
        without any thought of me

You don't knowingly
        hurt one you love

How could you do what
        you knew would hurt me

How could you throw away
years of togetherness
You say —
forgive me

I'm sorry
right now I can't
and
I can't say
I will ever be able to.

Please
　　don't ever disappear
　　　like that again.

I don't ever want to be
　　　lonely
　　　　　and
　　　　　　　alone
　　at the same time again

It's an experience
　　　　that not only drains you
but —
　　leaves you feeling helpless
　　　and yes —
　　　　　out of control

I missed you last night
　　　　and
　　　　　you were nowhere
　　　　　　to hear
　　　　　　to see
　　　　　　to touch
　　　　　　to hold

Please
　　Please
　　　come home.

This may sound strange
    but —
            I like silence

I like it when
            there is nothing to hear

Life is so filled
            with sound
                    with noise
            with thought interruptions

With noise that grabs
                    my ears
                        my eyes
                            my thought

I love it
    when I am alone
and
    can control the sounds
                    in my life

It seems that's the only time
            I can really enjoy me

For
　　　I've found that without that time
　　　　　I really don't
　　　　　　　enjoy others

Only when
　　　　I've had a time of silence
　　　are the sounds of others
　　　　　　a calming force
　　　and not
　　　　　　an interruption in my life

Yes, I like the sounds of silence
　　　they are the golden moments
　　　　　　　　of life.

Guess what
        I get to see you soon

It seems like a month
                since we have been together

I miss you so much
                        when
                I am away

It's like
        a part of me is missing
and
        that part is very vital

You know what
        I know I love you
but
        being away helps me
                to understand how much

It's hard
        to talk to you each night
                        on the phone
and not be able
                to see your expressions
                touch your words with my eyes
        watch your thoughts develop

You know what
        I get to see you soon
    my eyes get to meet yours
            my arms get to hold you
                    my body gets to feel yours

I think
    soon
            is too far away

Why can't soon
                be now

I miss you
    but
            I get to see you soon.

I

Thought
I

could
and tried

I

Knew
I

could

and
did

it

Thank you
    for the gifts you gave my life today

You gave me a smile
    when I couldn't find one

You gave me a song
    when my life was out of tune

You gave me your warmth
    when I felt damp from the cold of aloneness

You gave me a hug
    when I felt deserted

Thank you
    for the gift of you
        I wasn't expecting it
          but I'm glad
            it was there.

Do you know how I knew
you didn't want me

I left and you
didn't know
I was gone.

I wanted to talk
    but *I* was afraid
        they wouldn't listen

I wanted to scream
    but *I* was afraid
        they would tell me to shut-up

I wanted to cry
    but *I* was afraid
        they would think *I* was weak

So —
    I kept it all inside
        and hid it from them

Now —
    I'm hurting.

Wow —
    What a day
        Am I glad it's over

First, I couldn't get to sleep last night
    The pillows kept attacking me

Then —
    the alarm clock didn't go off
        I've never showered
            and dressed
        so quickly in my life

Then —
    I couldn't find the material
        the office had mailed

Finally at the bottom of the bell closet
    there it was

What else —
    The seminar started an hour late
        oh no —
            what do I cut out

This day isn't fair

Now the weather
    Fog everywhere
        airport maybe
            plane not sure

Why of all days today
    Hey up there
        Don't You Know

Tomorrow begins vacation
    You know I've been living for tomorrow

Come on —
    don't do this to me

Yea!
    Plane is here
        we're going

Watch out vacation
            here I come

Boy —
    Am I glad this day
        is almost over.

I can't begin to tell you
   how it hurts to watch them

I want to holler at them
   I want to shake them
      I want to scream
         WAKE-UP

I can't begin to tell you
   how much it hurts to listen to them

They never have any good to talk about
   They constantly put themselves down
      I want to scream
         LISTEN TO YOURSELF

Listen to how destructive you are to yourselves

What's wrong with people
   Why do people just give up
         Why won't they try

How can they become so satisfied
            in their self-destruction
   How have they become so beaten
            and self-defeated

Don't they know
      that life is a gift

59

Don't they care
        that they have no direction
    Don't they want to try

Don't they care
        that they are missing life
                Listen to me
            Life is now
                not where you've been

Life is now
        it's this moment
                Life is now
                    live it
                enjoy it
                        discover it

I know
        the bottom of the wall
                I've been there
but
        I refused to stay there
        I refused to drown

Even at the bottom
        I found you could still
                Look-up

Don't destroy yourself
            situations can't do it
                others can't do it
    You are the only one
    Look up —
            not down
        Look inside yourself —
                    not to others

Believe in you
            for you are a gift
        a unique person
                    a special event
    an adventure about to unfold
        You are worth the gold.

Oh little star
   could you help me

You are so far away
   yet each night you
      send your light to us

Oh little star
   could you help me

You see —
   I don't feel so bright tonight

Please tell me
   how do you do it
      how do you shine
         night after night

Don't you ever get tired
   of shining

Don't you ever get tired
   of always being on

Oh little star
   please let me learn from you

I'm tired of shining
    I'm tired of always having
        to be on

I want to turn off for a while
    I want to hide, behind
        the clouds

I want the sunshine to cover
            my escape

Oh, little star
    could you help me

Share with me
    your secret of brightness.

I can't stand it
    when you play games with me
I can't stand it
    when you play with my emotions
        my mind

And —
    don't tell me that
        you don't realize you're doing it

You know what you're doing

Why do you do that
    you know it hurts me
        don't you care

Sometimes I feel
        you want to hurt me

Why can't you
        just talk to me

I've told you before
        I can handle what I know
    it's the games
        it's the sarcasm
            it's the things you leave hanging
    that drive me crazy

Come on —

 let's stop the games
  let's stop the hurt
     let's stop the sarcasm
    let's go back to working together
   let's go back to pulling together
  let's go back to growing together
 let's stop the games
    they're destroying us.

What a neat day today was
for the first time in a while
we were alone

Alone without others
pulling at us
dividing us
questioning us

Alone
just you and I

Isn't it interesting
how we change
when we are alone

We seem so much more relaxed with each other
we're patient with our treatment

We're so much more considerate of each other
we don't bark as much

We're so much more caring with each other
we take time to touch with meaning

Know what I've decided
we need more time
alone with each other

We're so neat together
    when the world
            turns another direction
and
    we're alone.

Hello, wind
      would you come talk to me

Tell me

            where have you been
         what have you heard
      who have you seen

Say —
      could you stop pushing through
                        the trees
long enough
            to visit with me

Hello, wave
      would you come talk to me
tell me

            where have you been
         what have you heard
      who have you seen

Why do you have to hurry back
      you no sooner reach the shore
      and
            you're gone again

Could you stay around
                  a little longer

Why do things always seem to be
in a hurry

Why does life seem to rush
Why can't things slow down
so we can explore
can visit
can learn
from each other

Hello, life —
say
can we visit

Can you slow down long enough
for us to visit

Tell me
where have I been
what have I learned
who have I met
why am I rushing
and missing
getting to know me.

Thanks for talking with me
    Do you know how long it's been
        since I had someone
            who would talk with me

Most people want
        to talk to you
    not with you
                They want you
        to listen to them

They want your undivided attention
                        but —
            when they've said their piece

They don't want to listen
                they're finished

It doesn't matter
        that you need to talk

They don't have the time
    they won't give the energy

Thanks for talking with me
    it is so neat
        to have someone
            who listens
                who cares

Who responds with words
    that make sense
  that give meaning
   That explore
  That make you think

That don't always say
    what you want to hear

Thanks for talking with me
  it means so much
   to find one
  who doesn't just talk at you.

HUMAN

DICTIONARY

DREAM . . . . . .
a coloring book
for tomorrow.

ALONE . . . .
When your life is filled
with excitement
and
there is no one to tell.

PAIN . . . .
a knot in your
dental floss.

CROWD . . . .
one bathroom and four
daughters.

RAINBOW . . . . . .
finding the brilliance of color
in and through the lives of
others.

PANIC . . . .
> an unexpected surprise
> visit from your in-laws.

TORTURE . . . .
> when your in-laws decide
> to stay a few days longer.

TEMPORARY INSANITY . . . .
> when your in-laws
> decide to stay a
> second week.

HELL . . . .
> a fire in the area where there is no
> fire hydrant.

LOST . . . .
> a lack of direction when
> the street map has been clearly
> marked, but you can't read it.

CLOUDS ......

images that hinder your ability
to see the meaning above them.

HUG ....

a blanket that offers warmth from
the breeze of the day.

LIVING ....

Liking what you see
in the mirror
of your life.

SEXUAL FULFILLMENT ....

an inward explosion created
by an outward expression.

DIVORCE ....

a dead-end that is created because
we forget to follow the instructions.

TRUE FRIEND ....

one who holds the nail
while you hammer it.

MOTHER . . . .

The one who thought
you were beautiful
at your moment of birth.

FATHER . . . .

The one who agreed with
mother about your looks at
birth—even when he knew
it wasn't true.

FAMILY . . . .

Those who cared
enough to pick on you.

LOVER . . . .

that silent sense of completeness
expressed by another's body.

ENDING . . . .

the last piece of sun dropping
in the western sky.

RENEWAL. . . . . . .
    the sun bursting forth in the
    eastern sky.

WIND. . . . . . .
    a sense of aliveness that you
    can feel but not see.

SOLITUDE. . . . . . .
    the sound of the waves making
    their appearance upon the beach.

FRIEND. . . . . . .
    a hand that is volunteered
    before it is asked for.

BLINDNESS. . . . . . .
    When I shut my eyes
    to the things I should see,
    because of the fear of what
    I feel they might mean or
    ask me to do.

WINNER . . . .
One who finishes the race
with himself.

COMPANION . . . .
The right shoe
for the left foot.

WEALTH . . . .
Smiling because of
who you are —
not what you have.

GROWTH . . . .
Realizing that stature
is more important than
status.

PRAYERS

Lord,
    help me to understand
        that
            I can't give
                what I don't have
            I can't share
                what I've never felt
            I can't show
                what I've never seen
    help me to understand
        what I have
            where I've been
                what I've seen
        and —
            take those things
                and offer those
                    to others.

Lord,
　　would You do me
　　　　　　a special favor
　　Stay close to us
　　　　　　the next few days

You see
　　　　we've got some tough days
　　　　　　in front of us
　　Our relationship
　　　　is so vital to my life
　　　　　　　　but,
　　　　　　right now
　　　　we've got some real pressure

Grant us the freedom
　　　　to talk honestly
　　　　　　　openly
　　using the proper words
　　　　to express the inside

Grant us the ability to listen
　　　　　not with just emotional ears
　　but —
　　　　With concern,
　　　　　patience,
　　　　　　　gentleness
　　　　　　　and love.

Lord,
>   why can't I get her
>   out of my mind
>   out of my life

We've been apart for some time now
>   and —
>   she still haunts my life

I've prayed
>   and prayed
>   and it doesn't seem to help

Lord,
>   will I ever heal
>   will I ever turn loose
will I ever be free
>   of her space in my life

Please —
>   remove her
>   and help me
>   to get on with living.

Lord,
I know what the word
"no"
means
Just help me use it
at the right time.

Lord,

    thank You for each person
You bring into my life
May I never be too busy
    to experience the gift they are
there to give me.

Lord,
     Do You make house calls?

You see —
     I'm sick inside
           and,
          I'm not a good doctor
               for myself

I need someone
     who is more objective
          than I

For some reason
     I don't listen to myself.

Maybe,
    just maybe
I'm giving up too soon
Lord,
    please don't let me stop
        until every possible avenue
            has been explored
    until every possible thought
            has been examined

Lord,
    keep me restless
            until it's time
    then —
            only then
                grant me peace.

Lord,
	Help me to understand
that —
	I can't walk in Your shoes
but —
	I can learn from Your footprints.

Lord,
    I don't want
        to be a child again
    Just don't let me
        lose the child in me.

Lord,
    thank You for the stars
that show me
    that even in the midst of darkness
        there is still a ray of light.

Hey God —
    You're really neat
        When I think You're not there
            When I think You're not listening
    When I really feel that
            You're not aware of what's
              going on in my life
    You reveal Yourself,
            in the strangest ways

Thank You
    for hugging me today
        through the words of a friend.

Lord,
    I'm mad at You
        I asked You for something
            and,
                You didn't answer
    What do You mean
            You answered
    How could You have
          when
                I didn't get
        what I wanted.

Lord,
　　can I ask a special favor
　　　　stay close to her
　　　　　　this week
　　She's going to need You
　　　　The past months have been tough
　　　　　　but,
　　　　　　　this week

　　　　this week
　　　　will be the worst
　　She's going to have to leave
　　the last definition
　　　　of security
　　　　　she has had

Lord,
　　please hug her
　　　　in Your special way

She needs to know
　　that when things are gone

You
　　are still there.

Father,
I feel so bad
so lost

You see
she's hurting
and
I don't know
what to do
what to say
if to say

Lord,
I'm so confused
I really want to help
but,
I'm not sure how

Please
help her to know that
I care
let her know
I am her friend

I may not always know
what to say
but,
I really care.

Lord,
    may I ask You
    a personal question —

Do You ever get tired of being
    everyone's trash receptacle?

How do You do it —
    How do You carry the burdens
        of others?

I try Lord
    but,

        every now and then
it gets to me
        and I can't handle it

I wish I had Your patience
    Is that something You
        can teach me

I'd be willing to learn
    for —
        I want to help those
            who come to my life
        searching for direction

Lord,
    would You help me.

Lord,

we are gifts to each other
given by *You*
help us to not damage
what can be
help me to understand her wants
she comes from a world
I don't know

Thank You
for directing us.

Lord,
    I'm not sure
        how much longer
    I can keep this pace
    I'm here
        because
            You have placed me
                in this arena of service

Give me the strength
        to not only make the day,
but,
    be what You would have me be
        to each life
            that You share with me.

Lord —
   May my life be like that
      of a star
   Years after I've come home
         to You
   May my light still
         be seen by others.